Sheet Pan Cookbook

Blank Recipe Cookbook

My Recipe Journal

Why A Recipe Journal?

I know with all the technology today who really uses good old fashioned blank cookbooks, right?

Well, I do for one because by the time I am done trying to bookmark, download, share, copy and paste I could have just written it out by hand. Even if I successfully do any of those things the next time I want to make the recipe I have to hunt it down on my computer or in cyberland.

A hand written recipe book is something you can keep for a lifetime and I am sure more than one person reading this, has that cherished recipe book that has been handed down through the ages.

This book is meant to get dirty in the kitchen and be well used. The recipe book handed down to me is taped together and the writing is fading. I will be transferring all those recipes to a new book and retiring that one to a safe place. I guess you could call it a data transfer if you miss your techy feel.

You know what to do with this thing. Hunt down your favorite recipes on Pinterest or Facebook and write them in here. Log on to that computer and start writing those delicious bookmarked (soon to be deleted accidently in the next update) recipes out before you forget you even saw them in the first place.

Take this to your friend's house when they host a dinner party so you don't have to wait for them to email you the recipe (like that ever happens). Or you can just fill it with your own Frankenfood recipes. You know the ones that were amazing but you have no idea what you did. Now you will know exactly what to do next time just by using this handy blank recipe book.

Happy Eating!

Recipe Name

Page

_____   _____

_____   _____

_____   _____

_____   _____

_____   _____

_____   _____

_____   _____

_____   _____

_____   _____

_____   _____

_____   _____

_____   _____

_____   _____

_____   _____

Recipe Name

Page

_____ _____

_____ _____

_____ _____

_____ _____

_____ _____

_____ _____

_____ _____

_____ _____

_____ _____

_____ _____

_____ _____

_____ _____

_____ _____

_____ _____

Recipe Name   *Page #*

_____   _____

_____   _____

_____   _____

_____   _____

_____   _____

_____   _____

_____   _____

_____   _____

_____   _____

_____   _____

_____   _____

_____   _____

_____   _____

Recipe Name

Page #

_____   _____

_____   _____

_____   _____

_____   _____

_____   _____

_____   _____

_____   _____

_____   _____

_____   _____

_____   _____

_____   _____

_____   _____

_____   _____

_____   _____

Recipe Name

Page

_____   _____

_____   _____

_____   _____

_____   _____

_____   _____

_____   _____

_____   _____

_____   _____

_____   _____

_____   _____

_____   _____

_____   _____

_____   _____

_____   _____

Recipe Name

Page

_____ _____

_____ _____

_____ _____

_____ _____

_____ _____

_____ _____

_____ _____

_____ _____

_____ _____

Recipe Name: _____

Serving: _____ Prep. Time: _____ Cook Time: _____

Ingredients	**Directions**
_____	_____
_____	_____
_____	_____
_____	_____
_____	_____
_____	_____
_____	_____
_____	_____
_____	_____
_____	_____
_____	_____
_____	_____
_____	_____
_____	_____
_____	_____
_____	**Notes**
_____	_____
_____	_____
_____	_____

Cals: _____ Carbs: _____ Prot: _____ Fat: _____

Recipe Name: _____

Serving: _____ Prep. Time: _____ Cook Time: _____

Ingredients

_____

_____

_____

_____

_____

_____

_____

_____

_____

_____

_____

_____

_____

_____

_____

_____

_____

_____

_____

_____

Directions

_____

_____

_____

_____

_____

_____

_____

_____

_____

_____

_____

_____

_____

_____

_____

Notes

_____

_____

_____

Cals: _____   Carbs: _____   Prot: _____   Fat: _____

Recipe Name: _____

Serving:_____ Prep. Time: _____ Cook Time: _____

Ingredients

_____

_____

_____

_____

_____

_____

_____

_____

_____

_____

_____

_____

_____

_____

_____

_____

_____

_____

Directions

_____

_____

_____

_____

_____

_____

_____

_____

_____

_____

_____

_____

_____

_____

_____

Notes

_____

_____

_____

Cals: _____ Carbs: _____   Prot: _____ Fat: _____

Recipe Name: _____

Serving: _____ Prep. Time: _____ Cook Time: _____

Ingredients   ## Directions

_____   _____

_____   _____

_____   _____

_____   _____

_____   _____

_____   _____

_____   _____

_____   _____

_____   _____

_____   _____

_____   _____

_____   _____

_____   _____

_____   _____

_____   _____

_____   **Notes**

_____   _____

_____   _____

_____   _____

Cals: _____ Carbs: _____   Prot: _____ Fat: _____

Recipe Name: _____

Serving: _____ Prep. Time: _____ Cook Time: _____

Ingredients

_____

_____

_____

_____

_____

_____

_____

_____

_____

_____

_____

_____

_____

_____

_____

_____

_____

_____

_____

_____

Directions

_____

_____

_____

_____

_____

_____

_____

_____

_____

_____

_____

_____

_____

_____

_____

Notes

_____

_____

_____

Cals: _____ Carbs: _____   Prot: _____ Fat: _____

Recipe Name: _____

Serving:_____ Prep. Time: _____ Cook Time: _____

Ingredients   Directions

_____   _____

_____   _____

_____   _____

_____   _____

_____   _____

_____   _____

_____   _____

_____   _____

_____   _____

_____   _____

_____   _____

_____   _____

_____   _____

_____   _____

_____   _____

_____   **Notes**

_____   _____

_____   _____

_____   _____

Cals: _____ Carbs: _____ Prot: _____ Fat: _____

Recipe Name: _____

Serving: _____ Prep. Time: _____ Cook Time: _____

Ingredients

_____
_____
_____
_____
_____
_____
_____
_____
_____
_____
_____
_____
_____
_____
_____
_____
_____
_____

Directions

_____
_____
_____
_____
_____
_____
_____
_____
_____
_____
_____
_____
_____

Notes

_____
_____
_____

Cals: _____ Carbs: _____ Prot: _____ Fat: _____

Recipe Name: _____

Serving: _____ Prep. Time: _____ Cook Time: _____

Ingredients

_____
_____
_____
_____
_____
_____
_____
_____
_____
_____
_____
_____
_____
_____
_____
_____
_____
_____
_____
_____

Directions

_____
_____
_____
_____
_____
_____
_____
_____
_____
_____
_____
_____
_____
_____
_____
_____

Notes

_____
_____
_____

Cals: _____ Carbs: _____ Prot: _____ Fat: _____

Recipe Name: _____

Serving: _____ Prep. Time: _____ Cook Time: _____

Ingredients

_____

_____

_____

_____

_____

_____

_____

_____

_____

_____

_____

_____

_____

_____

_____

_____

_____

Directions

_____

_____

_____

_____

_____

_____

_____

_____

_____

_____

_____

_____

_____

Notes

_____

_____

_____

Cals: _____ Carbs: _____ Prot: _____ Fat: _____

Recipe Name: _____

Serving: _____ Prep. Time: _____ Cook Time: _____

Ingredients	**Directions**
_____	_____
_____	_____
_____	_____
_____	_____
_____	_____
_____	_____
_____	_____
_____	_____
_____	_____
_____	_____
_____	_____
_____	_____
_____	_____
_____	**Notes**
_____	_____
_____	_____
_____	_____

Cals: _____ Carbs: _____ Prot: _____ Fat: _____

Recipe Name: _____

Serving: _____ Prep. Time: _____ Cook Time: _____

Ingredients   ## Directions

_____   _____

_____   _____

_____   _____

_____   _____

_____   _____

_____   _____

_____   _____

_____   _____

_____   _____

_____   _____

_____   _____

_____   _____

_____   _____

_____   _____

_____   **Notes**

_____   _____

_____   _____

Cals: _____ Carbs: _____   Prot: _____ Fat: _____

Recipe Name: _____

Serving: _____ Prep. Time: _____ Cook Time: _____

Ingredients

_____

_____

_____

_____

_____

_____

_____

_____

_____

_____

_____

_____

_____

_____

_____

_____

_____

_____

Directions

_____

_____

_____

_____

_____

_____

_____

_____

_____

_____

_____

_____

_____

_____

Notes

_____

_____

_____

Cals: _____ Carbs: _____ Prot: _____ Fat: _____

Recipe Name: _____

Serving: _____ Prep. Time: _____ Cook Time: _____

Ingredients

_____

_____

_____

_____

_____

_____

_____

_____

_____

_____

_____

_____

_____

_____

_____

_____

_____

_____

Directions

_____

_____

_____

_____

_____

_____

_____

_____

_____

_____

_____

_____

_____

_____

Notes

_____

_____

_____

Cals: _____ Carbs: _____ Prot: _____ Fat: _____

Recipe Name: _____

Serving: _____ Prep. Time: _____ Cook Time: _____

Ingredients

_____
_____
_____
_____
_____
_____
_____
_____
_____
_____
_____
_____
_____
_____
_____
_____
_____
_____

Directions

_____
_____
_____
_____
_____
_____
_____
_____
_____
_____
_____
_____
_____
_____

Notes

_____
_____
_____

Cals: _____ Carbs: _____ Prot: _____ Fat: _____

Recipe Name: _____

Serving: _____ Prep. Time: _____ Cook Time: _____

Ingredients

_____

_____

_____

_____

_____

_____

_____

_____

_____

_____

_____

_____

_____

_____

_____

_____

_____

_____

Directions

_____

_____

_____

_____

_____

_____

_____

_____

_____

_____

_____

_____

_____

_____

Notes

_____

_____

_____

Cals: _____ Carbs: _____ Prot: _____ Fat: _____

Recipe Name: _____

Serving: _____ Prep. Time: _____ Cook Time: _____

Ingredients   ## Directions

_____   _____
_____   _____
_____   _____
_____   _____
_____   _____
_____   _____
_____   _____
_____   _____
_____   _____
_____   _____
_____   _____
_____   _____
_____   _____
_____   _____
_____   _____
_____

Notes

_____   _____
_____   _____
_____   _____

Cals: _____ Carbs: _____   Prot: _____ Fat: _____

Recipe Name: _____

Serving: _____ Prep. Time: _____ Cook Time: _____

Ingredients

_____

_____

_____

_____

_____

_____

_____

_____

_____

_____

_____

_____

_____

_____

_____

_____

_____

Directions

_____

_____

_____

_____

_____

_____

_____

_____

_____

_____

_____

_____

_____

_____

Notes

_____

_____

_____

Cals: _____ Carbs: _____   Prot: _____ Fat: _____

17

Recipe Name: _____

Serving: _____ Prep. Time: _____ Cook Time: _____

Ingredients

_____

_____

_____

_____

_____

_____

_____

_____

_____

_____

_____

_____

_____

_____

_____

_____

_____

_____

Directions

_____

_____

_____

_____

_____

_____

_____

_____

_____

_____

_____

_____

_____

_____

Notes

_____

_____

_____

Cals: _____ Carbs: _____ Prot: _____ Fat: _____

Recipe Name: _____

Serving: _____ Prep. Time: _____ Cook Time: _____

Ingredients

_____

_____

_____

_____

_____

_____

_____

_____

_____

_____

_____

_____

_____

_____

_____

_____

_____

_____

Directions

_____

_____

_____

_____

_____

_____

_____

_____

_____

_____

_____

_____

_____

_____

_____

Notes

_____

_____

_____

Cals: _____ Carbs: _____ Prot: _____ Fat: _____

Recipe Name: _____

Serving: _____ Prep. Time: _____ Cook Time: _____

Ingredients

_____
_____
_____
_____
_____
_____
_____
_____
_____
_____
_____
_____
_____
_____
_____
_____
_____
_____

Directions

_____
_____
_____
_____
_____
_____
_____
_____
_____
_____
_____
_____
_____

Notes

_____
_____
_____
_____

Cals: _____ Carbs: _____ Prot: _____ Fat: _____

Recipe Name: _____

Serving:_____Prep. Time: _____Cook Time:_____

Ingredients

_____

_____

_____

_____

_____

_____

_____

_____

_____

_____

_____

_____

_____

_____

_____

_____

_____

Directions

_____

_____

_____

_____

_____

_____

_____

_____

_____

_____

_____

_____

_____

_____

Notes

_____

_____

_____

Cals:_____   Carbs:_____   Prot:_____   Fat:_____

Recipe Name: _____

Serving: _____ Prep. Time: _____ Cook Time: _____

Ingredients

_____

_____

_____

_____

_____

_____

_____

_____

_____

_____

_____

_____

_____

_____

_____

_____

_____

_____

_____

_____

Directions

_____

_____

_____

_____

_____

_____

_____

_____

_____

_____

_____

_____

_____

_____

_____

_____

Notes

_____

_____

_____

Cals: _____ Carbs: _____   Prot: _____ Fat: _____

Recipe Name: _____

Serving: _____ Prep. Time: _____ Cook Time: _____

Ingredients   ## Directions

_____   _____

_____   _____

_____   _____

_____   _____

_____   _____

_____   _____

_____   _____

_____   _____

_____   _____

_____   _____

_____   _____

_____   _____

_____   ## Notes

_____   _____

_____   _____

_____   _____

Cals: _____   Carbs: _____   Prot: _____   Fat: _____

Recipe Name: _____

Serving: _____ Prep. Time: _____ Cook Time: _____

Ingredients	**Directions**
_____	_____
_____	_____
_____	_____
_____	_____
_____	_____
_____	_____
_____	_____
_____	_____
_____	_____
_____	_____
_____	_____
_____	_____
_____	_____
_____	**Notes**
_____	_____
_____	_____
_____	_____

Cals: _____ Carbs: _____ Prot: _____ Fat: _____

Recipe Name: _____

Serving: _____ Prep. Time: _____ Cook Time: _____

Ingredients

_____
_____
_____
_____
_____
_____
_____
_____
_____
_____
_____
_____
_____
_____
_____
_____
_____

Directions

_____
_____
_____
_____
_____
_____
_____
_____
_____
_____
_____
_____
_____
_____

Notes

_____
_____
_____

Cals: _____ Carbs: _____ Prot: _____ Fat: _____

Recipe Name: _____

Serving: _____ Prep. Time: _____ Cook Time: _____

Ingredients   ## Directions

_____   _____

_____   _____

_____   _____

_____   _____

_____   _____

_____   _____

_____   _____

_____   _____

_____   _____

_____   _____

_____   _____

_____   _____

_____   _____

_____   _____

_____   _____

_____   ## Notes

_____   _____

_____   _____

_____   _____

Cals: _____ Carbs: _____   Prot: _____ Fat: _____

Recipe Name: _____

Serving: _____ Prep. Time: _____ Cook Time: _____

Ingredients   ## Directions

_____   _____

_____   _____

_____   _____

_____   _____

_____   _____

_____   _____

_____   _____

_____   _____

_____   _____

_____   _____

_____   _____

_____   _____

_____   _____

_____   _____

_____   _____

_____   ### Notes

_____   _____

_____   _____

Cals: _____ Carbs: _____   Prot: _____ Fat: _____

Recipe Name: _____

Serving:_____ Prep. Time: _____ Cook Time: _____

Ingredients	**Directions**
_____	_____
_____	_____
_____	_____
_____	_____
_____	_____
_____	_____
_____	_____
_____	_____
_____	_____
_____	_____
_____	_____
_____	_____
_____	_____
_____	_____
_____	**Notes**
_____	_____
_____	_____
_____	_____

Cals:_____ Carbs: _____ Prot: _____ Fat: _____

Recipe Name: _____

Serving: _____ Prep. Time: _____ Cook Time: _____

Ingredients

Directions

_____   _____
_____   _____
_____   _____
_____   _____
_____   _____
_____   _____
_____   _____
_____   _____
_____   _____
_____   _____
_____   _____
_____   _____
_____   _____
_____   _____

Notes

_____   _____
_____   _____

Cals: _____ Carbs: _____   Prot: _____ Fat: _____

Recipe Name: _____

Serving: _____ Prep. Time: _____ Cook Time: _____

Ingredients

_____
_____
_____
_____
_____
_____
_____
_____
_____
_____
_____
_____
_____
_____
_____
_____
_____
_____

Directions

_____
_____
_____
_____
_____
_____
_____
_____
_____
_____
_____
_____
_____

Notes

_____
_____
_____

Cals: _____ Carbs: _____   Prot: _____ Fat: _____

Recipe Name: _____

Serving: _____ Prep. Time: _____ Cook Time: _____

Ingredients

_____
_____
_____
_____
_____
_____
_____
_____
_____
_____
_____
_____
_____
_____
_____
_____
_____

Directions

_____
_____
_____
_____
_____
_____
_____
_____
_____
_____
_____
_____
_____
_____

Notes

_____
_____
_____

Cals: _____ Carbs: _____   Prot: _____ Fat: _____

Recipe Name: _____

Serving: _____ Prep. Time: _____ Cook Time: _____

Ingredients

_____
_____
_____
_____
_____
_____
_____
_____
_____
_____
_____
_____
_____
_____
_____
_____
_____

Directions

_____
_____
_____
_____
_____
_____
_____
_____
_____
_____
_____
_____
_____

Notes

_____
_____
_____
_____

Cals: _____ Carbs: _____ Prot: _____ Fat: _____

Recipe Name: _____

Serving: _____ Prep. Time: _____ Cook Time: _____

Ingredients

_____

_____

_____

_____

_____

_____

_____

_____

_____

_____

_____

_____

_____

_____

_____

_____

_____

Directions

_____

_____

_____

_____

_____

_____

_____

_____

_____

_____

_____

_____

_____

_____

Notes

_____

_____

_____

Cals: _____ Carbs: _____ Prot: _____ Fat: _____

Recipe Name: _____

Serving:_____ Prep. Time: _____ Cook Time: _____

Ingredients

_____

_____

_____

_____

_____

_____

_____

_____

_____

_____

_____

_____

_____

_____

_____

_____

_____

_____

Directions

_____

_____

_____

_____

_____

_____

_____

_____

_____

_____

_____

_____

_____

Notes

_____

_____

_____

Cals: _____ Carbs: _____ Prot: _____ Fat: _____

Recipe Name: _____

Serving: _____ Prep. Time: _____ Cook Time: _____

Ingredients

Directions

_____

_____

_____

_____

_____

_____

_____

_____

_____

_____

_____

_____

_____

_____

_____

_____

_____

_____

Notes

_____

_____

_____

Cals: _____ Carbs: _____ Prot: _____ Fat: _____

Recipe Name: _____

Serving: _____ Prep. Time: _____ Cook Time: _____

Ingredients   ## Directions

_____   _____

_____   _____

_____   _____

_____   _____

_____   _____

_____   _____

_____   _____

_____   _____

_____   _____

_____   _____

_____   _____

_____   _____

_____   _____

_____   _____

_____   _____

_____   _____

_____   **Notes**

_____   _____

_____   _____

_____   _____

Cals: _____   Carbs: _____   Prot: _____   Fat: _____

Recipe Name: _____

Serving: _____ Prep. Time: _____ Cook Time: _____

Ingredients   ## Directions

_____   _____
_____   _____
_____   _____
_____   _____
_____   _____
_____   _____
_____   _____
_____   _____
_____   _____
_____   _____
_____   _____
_____   _____
_____   _____
_____   _____

Notes

_____   _____
_____   _____
_____   _____
_____   _____

Cals: _____ Carbs: _____   Prot: _____ Fat: _____

Recipe Name: _____

Serving: _____ Prep. Time: _____ Cook Time: _____

Ingredients

Directions

_____

_____

_____

_____

_____

_____

_____

_____

_____

_____

_____

_____

_____

_____

Notes

_____

_____

_____

Cals: _____ Carbs: _____   Prot: _____ Fat: _____

Recipe Name: _____

Serving: _____ Prep. Time: _____ Cook Time: _____

Ingredients

Directions

_____
_____
_____
_____
_____
_____
_____
_____
_____
_____
_____
_____
_____
_____
_____
_____
_____

Notes

Cals: _____ Carbs: _____ Prot: _____ Fat: _____

Recipe Name: _____

Serving: _____ Prep. Time: _____ Cook Time: _____

Ingredients

_____
_____
_____
_____
_____
_____
_____
_____
_____
_____
_____
_____
_____
_____
_____
_____
_____
_____

Directions

_____
_____
_____
_____
_____
_____
_____
_____
_____
_____
_____
_____
_____
_____

Notes

_____
_____
_____

Cals: _____ Carbs: _____ Prot: _____ Fat: _____

Recipe Name: _____

Serving: _____ Prep. Time: _____ Cook Time: _____

Ingredients

_____

_____

_____

_____

_____

_____

_____

_____

_____

_____

_____

_____

_____

_____

_____

_____

_____

_____

_____

_____

_____

Directions

_____

_____

_____

_____

_____

_____

_____

_____

_____

_____

_____

_____

_____

_____

_____

Notes

_____

_____

_____

Cals: _____ Carbs: _____ Prot: _____ Fat: _____

41

Recipe Name: _____

Serving: _____ Prep. Time: _____ Cook Time: _____

Ingredients

_____

_____

_____

_____

_____

_____

_____

_____

_____

_____

_____

_____

_____

_____

_____

_____

Directions

_____

_____

_____

_____

_____

_____

_____

_____

_____

_____

_____

_____

Notes

_____

_____

_____

Cals: _____ Carbs: _____ Prot: _____ Fat: _____

Recipe Name: _____

Serving: _____ Prep. Time: _____ Cook Time: _____

Ingredients   ## Directions

_____   _____
_____   _____
_____   _____
_____   _____
_____   _____
_____   _____
_____   _____
_____   _____
_____   _____
_____   _____
_____   _____
_____   _____
_____   _____
_____   _____
_____   _____
_____   **Notes**
_____   _____
_____   _____
_____   _____

Cals: _____ Carbs: _____   Prot: _____ Fat: _____

Recipe Name: _____

Serving: _____ Prep. Time: _____ Cook Time: _____

Ingredients

_____

_____

_____

_____

_____

_____

_____

_____

_____

_____

_____

_____

_____

_____

_____

_____

_____

_____

Directions

_____

_____

_____

_____

_____

_____

_____

_____

_____

_____

_____

_____

_____

_____

_____

Notes

_____

_____

_____

Cals: _____ Carbs: _____   Prot: _____ Fat: _____

Recipe Name: _____

Serving: _____ Prep. Time: _____ Cook Time: _____

Ingredients

_____

_____

_____

_____

_____

_____

_____

_____

_____

_____

_____

_____

_____

_____

_____

_____

_____

_____

Directions

_____

_____

_____

_____

_____

_____

_____

_____

_____

_____

_____

_____

_____

Notes

_____

_____

_____

Cals: _____ Carbs: _____ Prot: _____ Fat: _____

Recipe Name: _____

Serving: _____ Prep. Time: _____ Cook Time: _____

Ingredients

_____
_____
_____
_____
_____
_____
_____
_____
_____
_____
_____
_____
_____
_____
_____
_____
_____

Directions

_____
_____
_____
_____
_____
_____
_____
_____
_____
_____
_____
_____
_____
_____

Notes

_____
_____
_____
_____

Cals: _____ Carbs: _____ Prot: _____ Fat: _____

Recipe Name: _____

Serving: _____ Prep. Time: _____ Cook Time: _____

Ingredients

_____
_____
_____
_____
_____
_____
_____
_____
_____
_____
_____
_____
_____
_____
_____
_____
_____
_____
_____
_____

Directions

_____
_____
_____
_____
_____
_____
_____
_____
_____
_____
_____
_____
_____
_____
_____

Notes

_____
_____
_____

Cals: _____ Carbs: _____   Prot: _____ Fat: _____

Recipe Name: _____

Serving: _____ Prep. Time: _____ Cook Time: _____

Ingredients

_____
_____
_____
_____
_____
_____
_____
_____
_____
_____
_____
_____
_____
_____
_____
_____
_____
_____

Directions

_____
_____
_____
_____
_____
_____
_____
_____
_____
_____
_____
_____
_____

Notes

_____
_____
_____
_____

Cals: _____ Carbs: _____ Prot: _____ Fat: _____

Recipe Name: _____

Serving: _____ Prep. Time: _____ Cook Time: _____

Ingredients

_____
_____
_____
_____
_____
_____
_____
_____
_____
_____
_____
_____
_____
_____
_____
_____
_____
_____

Directions

_____
_____
_____
_____
_____
_____
_____
_____
_____
_____
_____
_____
_____
_____

Notes

_____
_____
_____

Cals: _____ Carbs: _____ Prot: _____ Fat: _____

Recipe Name: _____

Serving: _____ Prep. Time: _____ Cook Time: _____

Ingredients

_____

_____

_____

_____

_____

_____

_____

_____

_____

_____

_____

_____

_____

_____

_____

_____

_____

_____

_____

Directions

_____

_____

_____

_____

_____

_____

_____

_____

_____

_____

_____

_____

_____

_____

_____

_____

Notes

_____

_____

_____

Cals: _____ Carbs: _____ Prot: _____ Fat: _____

Recipe Name: _____

Serving: _____ Prep. Time: _____ Cook Time: _____

Ingredients

_____

_____

_____

_____

_____

_____

_____

_____

_____

_____

_____

_____

_____

_____

_____

_____

_____

_____

_____

Directions

_____

_____

_____

_____

_____

_____

_____

_____

_____

_____

_____

_____

_____

_____

_____

Notes

_____

_____

_____

Cals: _____ Carbs: _____ Prot: _____ Fat: _____

51

Recipe Name: _____

Serving: _____ Prep. Time: _____ Cook Time: _____

Ingredients

_____

_____

_____

_____

_____

_____

_____

_____

_____

_____

_____

_____

_____

_____

_____

Directions

_____

_____

_____

_____

_____

_____

_____

_____

_____

_____

_____

_____

_____

Notes

_____

_____

_____

Cals: _____ Carbs: _____ Prot: _____ Fat: _____

Recipe Name: _____

Serving:_____ Prep. Time: _____ Cook Time: _____

Ingredients

_____

_____

_____

_____

_____

_____

_____

_____

_____

_____

_____

_____

_____

_____

_____

_____

_____

Directions

_____

_____

_____

_____

_____

_____

_____

_____

_____

_____

_____

_____

_____

Notes

_____

_____

_____

Cals: _____ Carbs: _____   Prot: _____ Fat: _____

Recipe Name: _____

Serving: _____ Prep. Time: _____ Cook Time: _____

Ingredients

_____

_____

_____

_____

_____

_____

_____

_____

_____

_____

_____

_____

_____

_____

_____

_____

_____

_____

Directions

_____

_____

_____

_____

_____

_____

_____

_____

_____

_____

_____

_____

_____

_____

_____

Notes

_____

_____

_____

Cals: _____ Carbs: _____   Prot: _____ Fat: _____

Recipe Name: _____

Serving: _____ Prep. Time: _____ Cook Time: _____

Ingredients

_____

_____

_____

_____

_____

_____

_____

_____

_____

_____

_____

_____

_____

_____

_____

_____

_____

_____

Directions

_____

_____

_____

_____

_____

_____

_____

_____

_____

_____

_____

_____

_____

Notes

_____

_____

_____

Cals: _____ Carbs: _____   Prot: _____ Fat: _____

Recipe Name: _____

Serving: _____ Prep. Time: _____ Cook Time: _____

Ingredients

Directions

_____
_____
_____
_____
_____
_____
_____
_____
_____
_____
_____
_____
_____
_____
_____

Notes

_____
_____
_____

Cals: _____ Carbs: _____ Prot: _____ Fat: _____

Recipe Name: _____

Serving:_____ Prep. Time: _____ Cook Time: _____

Ingredients

_____

_____

_____

_____

_____

_____

_____

_____

_____

_____

_____

_____

_____

_____

_____

_____

Directions

_____

_____

_____

_____

_____

_____

_____

_____

_____

_____

_____

_____

_____

Notes

_____

_____

_____

Cals: _____ Carbs: _____   Prot: _____ Fat: _____

Recipe Name: _____

Serving: _____ Prep. Time: _____ Cook Time: _____

Ingredients

_____

_____

_____

_____

_____

_____

_____

_____

_____

_____

_____

_____

_____

_____

_____

_____

_____

_____

_____

Directions

_____

_____

_____

_____

_____

_____

_____

_____

_____

_____

_____

_____

_____

_____

_____

Notes

_____

_____

_____

Cals: _____ Carbs: _____   Prot: _____ Fat: _____

Recipe Name: _____

Serving: _____ Prep. Time: _____ Cook Time: _____

Ingredients

_____

_____

_____

_____

_____

_____

_____

_____

_____

_____

_____

_____

_____

_____

_____

_____

_____

_____

_____

Directions

_____

_____

_____

_____

_____

_____

_____

_____

_____

_____

_____

_____

_____

_____

_____

Notes

_____

_____

_____

Cals: _____ Carbs: _____   Prot: _____ Fat: _____

Recipe Name: _____

Serving:_____ Prep. Time: _____ Cook Time: _____

Ingredients	**Directions**
_____	_____
_____	_____
_____	_____
_____	_____
_____	_____
_____	_____
_____	_____
_____	_____
_____	_____
_____	_____
_____	_____
_____	_____
_____	_____
_____	_____
_____	**Notes**
_____	_____
_____	_____
_____	_____

Cals: _____ Carbs: _____   Prot: _____ Fat: _____

Recipe Name: _____

Serving: _____ Prep. Time: _____ Cook Time: _____

Ingredients

_____

_____

_____

_____

_____

_____

_____

_____

_____

_____

_____

_____

_____

_____

_____

_____

_____

_____

Directions

_____

_____

_____

_____

_____

_____

_____

_____

_____

_____

_____

_____

_____

_____

Notes

_____

_____

_____

Cals: _____ Carbs: _____ Prot: _____ Fat: _____

Recipe Name: _____

Serving: _____ Prep. Time: _____ Cook Time: _____

Ingredients   ## Directions

_____   _____
_____   _____
_____   _____
_____   _____
_____   _____
_____   _____
_____   _____
_____   _____
_____   _____
_____   _____
_____   _____
_____   _____
_____   _____
_____   _____
_____
_____   ### Notes
_____   _____
_____   _____
_____   _____

Cals: _____ Carbs: _____   Prot: _____ Fat: _____

Recipe Name: _____

Serving: _____ Prep. Time: _____ Cook Time: _____

Ingredients

_____

_____

_____

_____

_____

_____

_____

_____

_____

_____

_____

_____

_____

_____

_____

_____

_____

_____

_____

Directions

_____

_____

_____

_____

_____

_____

_____

_____

_____

_____

_____

_____

_____

_____

_____

Notes

_____

_____

_____

Cals: _____ Carbs: _____ Prot: _____ Fat: _____

63

Recipe Name: _____

Serving: _____ Prep. Time: _____ Cook Time: _____

Ingredients

_____

_____

_____

_____

_____

_____

_____

_____

_____

_____

_____

_____

_____

_____

_____

_____

_____

_____

Directions

_____

_____

_____

_____

_____

_____

_____

_____

_____

_____

_____

_____

_____

_____

Notes

_____

_____

_____

Cals: _____ Carbs: _____ Prot: _____ Fat: _____

Recipe Name: _____

Serving: _____ Prep. Time: _____ Cook Time: _____

Ingredients   ## Directions

_____   _____
_____   _____
_____   _____
_____   _____
_____   _____
_____   _____
_____   _____
_____   _____
_____   _____
_____   _____
_____   _____
_____   _____
_____   _____
_____   _____
_____   _____

Notes

_____   _____
_____   _____
_____   _____

Cals: _____ Carbs: _____   Prot: _____ Fat: _____

Recipe Name: _____

Serving: _____ Prep. Time: _____ Cook Time: _____

Ingredients

_____

_____

_____

_____

_____

_____

_____

_____

_____

_____

_____

_____

_____

_____

_____

_____

_____

_____

_____

_____

Directions

_____

_____

_____

_____

_____

_____

_____

_____

_____

_____

_____

_____

_____

_____

_____

_____

Notes

_____

_____

_____

_____

Cals: _____ Carbs: _____ Prot: _____ Fat: _____

Recipe Name: _____

Serving: _____ Prep. Time: _____ Cook Time: _____

Ingredients   ## Directions

_____   _____

_____   _____

_____   _____

_____   _____

_____   _____

_____   _____

_____   _____

_____   _____

_____   _____

_____   _____

_____   _____

_____   _____

_____   _____

_____   _____

_____   _____

_____   ### Notes

_____   _____

_____   _____

_____   _____

Cals: _____ Carbs: _____   Prot: _____ Fat: _____

Recipe Name: _____

Serving: _____ Prep. Time: _____ Cook Time: _____

Ingredients

_____
_____
_____
_____
_____
_____
_____
_____
_____
_____
_____
_____
_____
_____

Directions

_____
_____
_____
_____
_____
_____
_____
_____
_____
_____
_____
_____

Notes

_____
_____
_____

Cals: _____ Carbs: _____ Prot: _____ Fat: _____

Recipe Name: _____

Serving: _____ Prep. Time: _____ Cook Time: _____

Ingredients

Directions

_____

_____

_____

_____

_____

_____

_____

_____

_____

_____

_____

_____

_____

_____

_____

_____

_____

_____

_____

Notes

_____

_____

_____

Cals: _____ Carbs: _____ Prot: _____ Fat: _____

69

Recipe Name: _____

Serving: _____ Prep. Time: _____ Cook Time: _____

Ingredients

_____

_____

_____

_____

_____

_____

_____

_____

_____

_____

_____

_____

_____

_____

_____

_____

_____

_____

Directions

_____

_____

_____

_____

_____

_____

_____

_____

_____

_____

_____

_____

_____

_____

Notes

_____

_____

_____

_____

Cals: _____ Carbs: _____ Prot: _____ Fat: _____

Recipe Name: _____

Serving: _____ Prep. Time: _____ Cook Time: _____

Ingredients

_____

_____

_____

_____

_____

_____

_____

_____

_____

_____

_____

_____

_____

_____

_____

_____

_____

_____

Directions

_____

_____

_____

_____

_____

_____

_____

_____

_____

_____

_____

_____

_____

_____

Notes

_____

_____

_____

Cals: _____ Carbs: _____ Prot: _____ Fat: _____

Recipe Name: _____

Serving: _____ Prep. Time: _____ Cook Time: _____

Ingredients	**Directions**
_____	_____
_____	_____
_____	_____
_____	_____
_____	_____
_____	_____
_____	_____
_____	_____
_____	_____
_____	_____
_____	_____
_____	_____
_____	_____
_____	_____
_____	**Notes**
_____	_____
_____	_____
_____	_____

Cals: _____ Carbs: _____   Prot: _____ Fat: _____

Recipe Name: _____

Serving: _____ Prep. Time: _____ Cook Time: _____

Ingredients

_____

_____

_____

_____

_____

_____

_____

_____

_____

_____

_____

_____

_____

_____

_____

_____

_____

_____

Directions

_____

_____

_____

_____

_____

_____

_____

_____

_____

_____

_____

_____

_____

_____

Notes

_____

_____

_____

Cals: _____ Carbs: _____ Prot: _____ Fat: _____

Recipe Name: _____

Serving: _____ Prep. Time: _____ Cook Time: _____

Ingredients	Directions
_____	_____
_____	_____
_____	_____
_____	_____
_____	_____
_____	_____
_____	_____
_____	_____
_____	_____
_____	_____
_____	_____
_____	_____
_____	_____
_____	**Notes**
_____	_____
_____	_____
_____	_____

Cals: _____ Carbs: _____ Prot: _____ Fat: _____

Recipe Name: _____

Serving: _____ Prep. Time: _____ Cook Time: _____

Ingredients

Directions

_____

_____

_____

_____

_____

_____

_____

_____

_____

_____

_____

_____

_____

_____

_____

_____

_____

_____

_____

_____

Notes

_____

_____

_____

Cals: _____ Carbs: _____ Prot: _____ Fat: _____

Recipe Name: _____

Serving: _____ Prep. Time: _____ Cook Time: _____

Ingredients   ## Directions

_____   _____
_____   _____
_____   _____
_____   _____
_____   _____
_____   _____
_____   _____
_____   _____
_____   _____
_____   _____
_____   _____
_____   _____
_____   _____
_____   _____
_____   _____

Notes

_____   _____
_____   _____
_____   _____

Cals: _____ Carbs: _____   Prot: _____ Fat: _____

Recipe Name: _____

Serving: _____ Prep. Time: _____ Cook Time: _____

Ingredients   ## Directions

_____   _____

_____   _____

_____   _____

_____   _____

_____   _____

_____   _____

_____   _____

_____   _____

_____   _____

_____   _____

_____   _____

_____   _____

_____   _____

_____   _____

_____   _____

_____   ### Notes

_____   _____

_____   _____

_____   _____

Cals: _____ Carbs: _____   Prot: _____ Fat: _____

Recipe Name: _____

Serving: _____ Prep. Time: _____ Cook Time: _____

Ingredients

_____

_____

_____

_____

_____

_____

_____

_____

_____

_____

_____

_____

_____

_____

_____

_____

_____

_____

_____

Directions

_____

_____

_____

_____

_____

_____

_____

_____

_____

_____

_____

_____

_____

_____

_____

_____

Notes

_____

_____

_____

Cals: _____ Carbs: _____ Prot: _____ Fat: _____

Recipe Name: _____

Serving: _____ Prep. Time: _____ Cook Time: _____

Ingredients

_____

_____

_____

_____

_____

_____

_____

_____

_____

_____

_____

_____

_____

_____

_____

_____

_____

_____

_____

_____

Directions

_____

_____

_____

_____

_____

_____

_____

_____

_____

_____

_____

_____

_____

_____

_____

Notes

_____

_____

_____

Cals: _____ Carbs: _____ Prot: _____ Fat: _____

Recipe Name: _____

Serving: _____ Prep. Time: _____ Cook Time: _____

Ingredients

_____
_____
_____
_____
_____
_____
_____
_____
_____
_____
_____
_____
_____
_____
_____
_____
_____
_____
_____

Directions

_____
_____
_____
_____
_____
_____
_____
_____
_____
_____
_____
_____
_____
_____
_____

Notes

_____
_____
_____
_____

Cals: _____ Carbs: _____ Prot: _____ Fat: _____

Recipe Name: _____

Serving: _____ Prep. Time: _____ Cook Time: _____

Ingredients

_____

_____

_____

_____

_____

_____

_____

_____

_____

_____

_____

_____

_____

_____

_____

_____

_____

Directions

_____

_____

_____

_____

_____

_____

_____

_____

_____

_____

_____

_____

_____

_____

Notes

_____

_____

_____

Cals: _____ Carbs: _____ Prot: _____ Fat: _____

Recipe Name: _____

Serving: _____ Prep. Time: _____ Cook Time: _____

Ingredients

Directions

_____

_____

_____

_____

_____

_____

_____

_____

_____

_____

_____

_____

_____

_____

_____

_____

_____

_____

_____

_____

_____

_____

_____

_____

_____

_____

_____

_____

_____

_____

Notes

_____

_____

_____

_____

Cals: _____ Carbs: _____   Prot: _____ Fat: _____

Recipe Name: _____

Serving: _____ Prep. Time: _____ Cook Time: _____

Ingredients

_____

_____

_____

_____

_____

_____

_____

_____

_____

_____

_____

_____

_____

_____

_____

_____

_____

_____

_____

Directions

_____

_____

_____

_____

_____

_____

_____

_____

_____

_____

_____

_____

_____

_____

Notes

_____

_____

_____

Cals: _____ Carbs: _____   Prot: _____ Fat: _____

Recipe Name: _____

Serving: _____ Prep. Time: _____ Cook Time: _____

Ingredients

_____

_____

_____

_____

_____

_____

_____

_____

_____

_____

_____

_____

_____

_____

_____

_____

_____

_____

Directions

_____

_____

_____

_____

_____

_____

_____

_____

_____

_____

_____

_____

_____

Notes

_____

_____

_____

Cals: _____ Carbs: _____ Prot: _____ Fat: _____

Recipe Name: _____

Serving:_____ Prep. Time: _____ Cook Time: _____

Ingredients

Directions

_____
_____
_____
_____
_____
_____
_____
_____
_____
_____
_____
_____
_____
_____
_____
_____
_____
_____
_____

Notes

_____
_____
_____
_____

Cals: _____ Carbs: _____ Prot: _____ Fat: _____

Recipe Name: _____

Serving: _____ Prep. Time: _____ Cook Time: _____

Ingredients

_____
_____
_____
_____
_____
_____
_____
_____
_____
_____
_____
_____
_____
_____
_____
_____
_____
_____

Directions

_____
_____
_____
_____
_____
_____
_____
_____
_____
_____
_____
_____
_____

Notes

_____
_____
_____

Cals: _____ Carbs: _____ Prot: _____ Fat: _____

Recipe Name: _____

Serving: _____ Prep. Time: _____ Cook Time: _____

Ingredients

_____
_____
_____
_____
_____
_____
_____
_____
_____
_____
_____
_____
_____
_____
_____
_____
_____
_____

Directions

_____
_____
_____
_____
_____
_____
_____
_____
_____
_____
_____
_____
_____

Notes

_____
_____
_____

Cals: _____ Carbs: _____   Prot: _____ Fat: _____

Recipe Name: _____

Serving: _____ Prep. Time: _____ Cook Time: _____

Ingredients	**Directions**
_____	_____
_____	_____
_____	_____
_____	_____
_____	_____
_____	_____
_____	_____
_____	_____
_____	_____
_____	_____
_____	_____
_____	_____
_____	_____
_____	**Notes**
_____	_____
_____	_____
_____	_____

Cals: _____ Carbs: _____ Prot: _____ Fat: _____

Recipe Name: _____

Serving: _____ Prep. Time: _____ Cook Time: _____

Ingredients

_____

_____

_____

_____

_____

_____

_____

_____

_____

_____

_____

_____

_____

_____

_____

_____

_____

_____

_____

Directions

_____

_____

_____

_____

_____

_____

_____

_____

_____

_____

_____

_____

_____

_____

_____

_____

Notes

_____

_____

_____

Cals: _____ Carbs: _____ Prot: _____ Fat: _____

Recipe Name: _____

Serving: _____ Prep. Time: _____ Cook Time: _____

Ingredients   Directions

_____   _____

_____   _____

_____   _____

_____   _____

_____   _____

_____   _____

_____   _____

_____   _____

_____   _____

_____   _____

_____   _____

_____   _____

_____   _____

_____   _____

_____   _____

Notes

_____   _____

_____   _____

_____   _____

Cals: _____ Carbs: _____   Prot: _____ Fat: _____

Recipe Name: _____

Serving: _____ Prep. Time: _____ Cook Time: _____

Ingredients

_____

_____

_____

_____

_____

_____

_____

_____

_____

_____

_____

_____

_____

_____

_____

_____

_____

_____

_____

_____

Directions

_____

_____

_____

_____

_____

_____

_____

_____

_____

_____

_____

_____

_____

_____

_____

Notes

_____

_____

_____

Cals: _____ Carbs: _____   Prot: _____ Fat: _____

Recipe Name: _____

Serving: _____ Prep. Time: _____ Cook Time: _____

Ingredients

_____

_____

_____

_____

_____

_____

_____

_____

_____

_____

_____

_____

_____

_____

_____

_____

_____

_____

_____

Directions

_____

_____

_____

_____

_____

_____

_____

_____

_____

_____

_____

_____

_____

_____

_____

Notes

_____

_____

_____

Cals: _____ Carbs: _____ Prot: _____ Fat: _____

Recipe Name: _____

Serving: _____ Prep. Time: _____ Cook Time: _____

Ingredients

_____

_____

_____

_____

_____

_____

_____

_____

_____

_____

_____

_____

_____

_____

_____

_____

_____

Directions

_____

_____

_____

_____

_____

_____

_____

_____

_____

_____

_____

_____

_____

Notes

_____

_____

_____

Cals: _____ Carbs: _____ Prot: _____ Fat: _____

Recipe Name: _____

Serving: _____ Prep. Time: _____ Cook Time: _____

Ingredients

_____

_____

_____

_____

_____

_____

_____

_____

_____

_____

_____

_____

_____

_____

_____

_____

_____

Directions

_____

_____

_____

_____

_____

_____

_____

_____

_____

_____

_____

_____

_____

_____

Notes

_____

_____

_____

Cals: _____ Carbs: _____ Prot: _____ Fat: _____

Recipe Name: _____

Serving: _____ Prep. Time: _____ Cook Time: _____

Ingredients

_____

_____

_____

_____

_____

_____

_____

_____

_____

_____

_____

_____

_____

_____

_____

_____

_____

_____

_____

Directions

_____

_____

_____

_____

_____

_____

_____

_____

_____

_____

_____

_____

_____

_____

_____

Notes

_____

_____

_____

Cals: _____ Carbs: _____ Prot: _____ Fat: _____

Recipe Name: _____

Serving: _____ Prep. Time: _____ Cook Time: _____

Ingredients

_____

_____

_____

_____

_____

_____

_____

_____

_____

_____

_____

_____

_____

_____

_____

Directions

_____

_____

_____

_____

_____

_____

_____

_____

_____

_____

_____

Notes

_____

_____

_____

Cals: _____ Carbs: _____ Prot: _____ Fat: _____

Recipe Name: _____

Serving: _____ Prep. Time: _____ Cook Time: _____

Ingredients

_____

_____

_____

_____

_____

_____

_____

_____

_____

_____

_____

_____

_____

_____

_____

_____

_____

_____

Directions

_____

_____

_____

_____

_____

_____

_____

_____

_____

_____

_____

_____

_____

_____

_____

Notes

_____

_____

_____

Cals: _____ Carbs: _____ Prot: _____ Fat: _____

Recipe Name: _____

Serving: _____ Prep. Time: _____ Cook Time: _____

Ingredients

_____

_____

_____

_____

_____

_____

_____

_____

_____

_____

_____

_____

_____

_____

Directions

_____

_____

_____

_____

_____

_____

_____

_____

_____

_____

_____

Notes

_____

_____

_____

Cals: _____ Carbs: _____ Prot: _____ Fat: _____

Recipe Name: _____

Serving: _____ Prep. Time: _____ Cook Time: _____

Ingredients

_____

_____

_____

_____

_____

_____

_____

_____

_____

_____

_____

_____

_____

_____

_____

_____

_____

_____

_____

Directions

_____

_____

_____

_____

_____

_____

_____

_____

_____

_____

_____

_____

_____

_____

Notes

_____

_____

_____

Cals: _____ Carbs: _____   Prot: _____ Fat: _____

Recipe Name: _____

Serving: _____ Prep. Time: _____ Cook Time: _____

Ingredients

_____

_____

_____

_____

_____

_____

_____

_____

_____

_____

_____

_____

_____

_____

Directions

_____

_____

_____

_____

_____

_____

_____

_____

_____

_____

Notes

_____

_____

_____

Cals: _____ Carbs: _____ Prot: _____ Fat: _____

A Blank Book Billionaire Creation

CPSIA information can be obtained
at www.ICGtesting.com
Printed in the USA
LVOW04s0929150118

562979LV00037B/2152/P